# For the Greek Spring

"Amasis' reign is said to have marked a high point in Egypt's fortunes in terms of what the river gave to the land and what the land gave to the people... Moreover, it was Amasis who ordained that every year every Egyptian should divulge how he made a living to the governor of his province, and decreed the death penalty for anyone who failed to do this or who could not show he made a living in an honest fashion. Solon of Athens took this law over from Egypt and made it part of the legal system in Athens, where they should let it remain in force for ever, because it is an excellent law."

Herodotus 2.177.
*Translated Robin Waterfield, Carolyn Dewald.*

*Also by Kelvin Corcoran*

Robin Hood in the Dark Ages
The Red and Yellow Book
Qiryat Sepher
TCL
The Next Wave
Lyric Lyric
Melanie's Book
When Suzy Was
Your Thinking Tracts or Nations
New and Selected Poems
Roger Hilton's Sugar
Backward Turning Sea
Hotel Shadow

*For the Greek Spring*

Kelvin Corcoran

Shearsman Books

First published in the United Kingdom in 2013 by
Shearsman Books
50 Westons Hill Drive
Emersons Green
BRISTOL
BS16 7DF

Shearsman Books Ltd Registered Office
30–31 St. James Place, Mangotsfield, Bristol BS16 9JB
(this address not for correspondence)

www.shearsman.com

ISBN 978-1-84861-276-1

Copyright © Kelvin Corcoran, 2000, 2004, 2007, 2010, 2013.
The right of Kelvin Corcoran to be identified as the author
of this work has been asserted by him in accordance with the
Copyrights, Designs and Patents Act of 1988.
All rights reserved.

Acknowledgements
Many of the poems appearing in this volume were
previously published in the following books:
*When Suzy Was* (Shearsman Books, 2000), *New and Selected Poems* (Shearsman, 2004), *Backward Turning Sea* (Shearsman, 2007), *Hotel Shadow* (Shearsman, 2010). With thanks to Brian Lewis and philip kuhn respectively, 'Four Voices From' was first published in *Words Through A Hole Where Once There Was A Chimpanzee's Face*, Longbarrow Press, 2011, and an earlier version of the first part of 'Sea Table' was published by itinerant press, 2012.

Cover painting by Peter Hughes.

# Contents

### Occurrences of the Name Helen
| | |
|---|---|
| *From here according to Jenkyns* | 9 |
| Hotel Byron | 10 |
| Helen Mania | 13 |
| *After the final mountains* | 19 |
| Epicurus Is My Neighbour | 20 |
| The Harbour at Night | 24 |
| Four Voices From | 25 |
| *Over the calm, clear shining water* | 28 |

### At the Centre of the World
| | |
|---|---|
| At the Centre of the World | 35 |
| The Name Apollo | 36 |
| The Roadside Shrine | 38 |
| The Artemision Tunnel | 41 |
| Interview | 42 |
| My Journey to Euripides | 43 |
| From Alexiares' Notebooks | 48 |
| Alexiares In Exile | 52 |

### Myriorama
| | |
|---|---|
| Sea Table | 61 |
| Three Monologues | 70 |
| Myriorama | 77 |
| Ambelakia | 80 |
| The Objects Were Not Paid For | 81 |
| *Early morning frost* | 82 |
| Disclaimer | 83 |
| From the Harbour | 84 |
| Byron's Karagiozis | 87 |
| Apokriatika | 92 |
| News of Aristomenes | 95 |

### On the Xenophone Label
| | |
|---|---|
| Propositions 1 | 115 |
| A Biography of Xenophanes | 118 |

| | |
|---|---|
| Greetings 1 | 119 |
| Biography 2 | 121 |
| Propositions 2 | 122 |
| Biography 3 | 125 |
| Greetings 2 | 126 |
| Biography 4 | 128 |
| The End of It All | 129 |
| Propositions 3 | 130 |
| | |
| Notes | 134 |

# Occurrences of the Name Helen

## *From here according to Jenkyns*

From here according to Jenkyns
Sappho entered the western lyric;
I can see the coast of Asia minor,
low blue hills, an apron of light.

The water's not wide, though I can't
get o'er dark imperial Anatolia
where my language was made;
aconite, mallow, fennel at the root.

# Hotel Byron

From Hotel Byron the wind slips over red tiled roofs
bearing us back into port, one more day.
The red and black banners of the KKE
stretched tight as sails above each street,
—they think Lenin lives still in Moscow,
nobody tells them, so they think it still.

Above the sea, a village of old people,
—You Italiani? America? No, Anglos.
No bakery here, at night the dark sea speaks;
no pirates, no Turks, no baker.

Our faces sunk in Saronic blue,
we suffered confusion, the last car fading.
Small boats scud and arc across the bay of light
and you make those shapes with your mouth that I love.

*

Laconic

Kranai     Marathonisi     isle of fennel
one fisherman     the still waters of Githyon
the sun rising

Kranai, Helen said, so
tell me now and I won't ask again
and with morning they sailed into myth.

*

The choir of many voices sing
my heart is broken, oh
the bird flies from the clearing.

How one sound, all my life I've heard
our mouths close around many shapes
possessed by death, by vengeance song.

Deepest octosyllabic land
oh my heart is, the sea rages
make me see what's in front of my face.

\*

In the fast channel of Despotikon
I married the sea, the gold circle sank
to surface in a dream all night.
Out of corrugated light; give it back.

Its white absence aches on my finger,
stolen from sense to the sea bed.
If I could work it out
I would know you again.

There is:
the apparent surface of the water;
the light in the body of the water;
the unknown ground under the water.

It sank because it was an object.
It cannot be lost, love has no weight.
It sank into irretrievable regret.
Give it back.

\*

By Monday, at the end of the world,
falling in the dizzy air of Cape Matepan,
the lighthouse, the cornflowers alight like blue sparks,
no birds calling the last step down

drowns us into the submarine cave called hell.
You can get into hell. It's not literature.

Each separate light a white path on the sliding waves.

At the end of the world, ships pass bound for Crete,
blue devices low in the water following a strange trade.
We lost track of days and the meaning of number,
heads empty to the waves speaking the first language of sense;
island to island white spume ripples the shore,
a whole country rising up in free association.

## Helen Mania

Yannis told us of the alternative escape route,
Helen and Paris making chariot wheel tracks in Thalami
down to the harbour at Pephnos.

Spartans left waiting at Kranai,
mouths open, bored before the myth
—look at those sparks, like stars eh?

They spent their first night here,
fell upon one another, spent
until the sun came over Taygetos.

Helen set foot on board, trumpets sound
over water, sewing in the grain
the ships of all the world in her wake.

*

Helen didn't want the trouble
safe behind those walls
the army of the fertile plain said so.

I looked at Marathonisi, plotted
the chariot tracks crashing down
from Thalami to Pephnos and the sea.

Helen didn't want it to happen,
then love like Paris arrived.

I looked at the serene harbour
isle of fennel, empty blue mirror,
Helen was not there nor in Egypt.

Honey melting the other side of Taygetos that night.

*

We need a name for this war,
economics won't move our heroes;
plunder is nearer to it but
join our trade war won't swing it.

We need to make it personal.
Control of grain ships through the straights
and increased tax revenue? I think not;
if we had a woman abducted for instance.

In the future they'll see through us,
as if we would turn the world upside down
for a Spartan girl who warmed up the house guest?
Menelaus' hot wife gone wrong.

\*

I set my foot in the track
greased slot to smashed Ilium,
one way ride to bliss or exile.

Night of stars, night of revelation
silver jackal sniffing around the door,
storm came smoking off Taygetos.

The house became a boat and
the great green flooded her mind
the island, her dream, floated out to Paris.

Snakes and figs littered the yard.

That morning Helen threw aside the carpet of stars,
that morning Helen stepped aboard.

\*

I kept my Spartan girl wrapped up,
hidden under a pile of cloaks
for this languid, sexual periplus.

We drew bright lines across the water
phosphor alphabet dissolving clues,
we lipsticked the mouth of hell below Tanaeron.

Even so she could not be dimmed,
she shone so fair like a bowl of light
desire lifted us like the tide.

Up from the inky black a message,
where fish pick the bones clean and
fields of seaweed denote a continent.

We turned the world upside down:
Menelaus—Where are your divisions now? Stop.
—Your squad cars and riches? Stop.

I left of my own freewill and cannot stop. Stop.

She lay in the boat burning, my beacon,
shaped by heaven,
they built temples in her wake.

*

Who would believe it over a girl?
despite our endless back and forth,
Io, Europa, Medea and the sassy east?
Moon-struck lovers is all we need.

We could get the Egyptian priests on our side,
build a temple to the goddess stranger;
variation as a post-something aesthetic,
she was a ghost above the Skaian gates etc.

I have it now: our brother's loss is our cause.
Make sure you don't catch them,
clear all the harbours down to Matepan;
it's Priam's turn for regime change.

*

We fled in the hour of the furnace
Helen a black outline in the blast
dark one, I see only your face.

Swing the pendulum myth
another woman, another man sail eastward
pass Cythera, ploughing the grain.

Aphrodite came swanning out
attendant gods swim in her wake,
their mouths shaping O O in the eddies.

Oh Helen I loved every woman
to have you, Mr Meat Me, the fool
to find you deep in darkness.

*

My lord they have flown;
I have posted guards to the passes
but who can outrun love?
I'll stick the barb into Menelaus.

I think I hear armour clashing by night,
see smart bomb snapshots of Trojan bunkers;
saturation red hits the air in waves,
reconstructed it's just as real.

Draw up the list of ships
and tilt our western powers into the east;

we can lead our little princes
into the divided meadows of Aphrodite.

*

Helen you are not to blame,
your smoky heart faced the east
the colour rising inside you.

She ascends the steps above the gate,
Helen, the cicadas whisper unearthly,
the sky fuses around the shape of a girl.

Politicians made silent as stone,
remember hope, scratch at lust,
the word wanton dry in their mouths.

She steps forward parting the air
into the live broadcast
wrapped around the world.

She steps forward, pictures the boat
parting the waves, the field of men below,
what? the dream of? the plains of Argos?

She wanted to see her brothers
on the island of Pephnos, they stand in the waves,
guarding the safe passage of her escape.

She steps forward, it is Helen
ascending, her shape makes a window
in the air for the breathless sky.

*

We saw the sun burn the high meadows
the rain drench the white roots
the wind fuck the come hither waves.

We ran up the goat tracks, breathless
between spurge and aconite and mallow.

Helen you have undone the world
I taste your looks, touch your colour
you were always there, my radiant lexicon.

See how our boat dips and rises
to our shared step aboard
noses out of Pephnos over the endless sea.

We lie together in the seabed
just rippling the light with our breath.

## *After the final mountains we roll down to the sea*

After the final mountains we roll down to the sea
south from Kalamata around Taygetos on the Aeriopoli road,
and this is meant to be the literal poem of that journey,
one of a series joining seven songs in transit
as if your whole life comes in on the glimmering tide.

The road turns in a certain way and you see everything,
along this coast where gods and babies are washed ashore
out of the sky into the doorways of abandoned villages;
you can pull up and buy oranges, potatoes, honey
from the last ones alive in unpopulated places.

In the meadows and olive groves myth takes root,
paths in the hills lead there, if you can crawl and scramble;
the snake renews itself and polyphonous birds call,
strophe by strophe in the month of fair sailing
the world takes off to a single tone breaking underground.

The road turns in a certain way—miss it and you die;
ceremonies lift the earth people, gibbering at the edge,
and the voice from the well asks—what do you want?
The route is lined with bright and useless answers,
as if anything could keep us from the great descent.

Where the land ends Helen's brothers look out for us,
striding over the contours of the sea, they say;
as candid waves explode on harbour walls
a girl from Cythera rises, from the epicentre,
to leave us drenched and shining in shock.

## Epicurus Is My Neighbour

He was the son of economic migrants,
the borders had holes in then, the bosses forgetful;
there were compensations on Samos—and fish.

He recruited his brothers as his first adherents,
and seeking undisturbedness he travelled widely:
Samos; Athens; Colophon; Mytilene and Lampsacus.

A car lights the dark road running,
we thought of the towns out there, subtle objects
in motion—the infinite as absence of collision.

Epicurus walked out on nonsense and uncaring gods,
let it come to us by this light, he sat in his garden,
written on carbonised papyrus, chipped in stone.

\*

We're walking by the sea Melanie,
the sea's full of stories, wavering and drunk,
the olive trees whirl and stars like spilt milk.

The light slides over the water once only,
below it's dark, all the way down unthinkable,
—so don't think about it then, you'd say.

Let's walk to the house, it's after the next turn,
the air fit medium for the colour shift of night.

\*

Epicurus stands at the door of the sea,
he fixes his mouth in place, sea-foam
forms an outline like fuzzy television,
the trick is to read it as a poem.

I'm not making this up, Epicurus
waits for the fat snow to fall,
to calculate the disposition of the flakes
the dance of sensory data around the world.

*

Another night in, storm rocking the lamp
the red wine I think, roast potatoes, onion,
readings from Lucretius and a slight moon;
the sky falling away like a dreaming face,
a girl's face looking out to sea, eyes open.

We drove down through swirling fog,
Langada, Thalames, the mountain made invisible,
the roads in Sparta like black rivers run,
a Spring tide of black glass splintering
the roots and names of big gods and little gods.

With morning up early for Clean Monday
the kites sail high as white on blue,
a white word disintegrating the whole sky
keeps us fed, makes us free, let's me sit here
and stare at the green gate to the sea.

*

I saw a completeness
it made sense I was
a boy and it was death
I saw their faces

but would not step
away please not yet
then my girls then
two women looking down

but would not step
away please not yet
then my girls then
two women looking down

I saw a completeness
it made sense I was
a boy and it was death
I saw their faces

*

Herodotus before you run me down in Athens
let me give you a summary of my system.
Ataraxia: I've stretched it on a banner across the street
                    ATARAXIA
for all to pass under and gaze upon in wonder.

There's no point in using words that make no sense,
that are unattached to the world; we know it, everyday
we know it, that's apparent despite the same old business;
look at the boundless sky—and my banner,
look at boundlessness at every turn, bodies and void.

                *

The wind blows and the house stands,
the roof holds and I see us lie under it;
I see the garden thrashing all night and
the village launch itself into deep water,
the wind rolling off the sea explodes thought.

In mountain clamour the high meadows
blown white and bare detonate particles at swim
against our silver window, a lexicon
smashed and scattered uncoded bright beads
remaking the swept world by morning.

Mountains rise in the empty box of the sky,
the fresh green smell of sap fills the air
and if there's talk around here, it won't trouble
the stealthy ships of an unknown country
rounding the headland in silence.

                *

a body of fine particles
dispersed
            furthermore

the birds in the bare tree
the birds in the green leafy

furthermore
the mode of investigation counts

attend to the visible
a bound or outer limit set

a single account is the business of those
who wish to perform marvels for the rabble

Thales invented water—Epicurus ease
he danced with Lucretius

## The Harbour at Night

In Agios Dimitrios the faultline sounds,
the radio plays and the last car I know
the language of birds calling;
Pephnos rises, Malovos of the shadows appears
and the harbour is an amphitheatre of air.

Open to the west, the sea glitters hidden light,
the fishing boat passes where the dioskouroi stand;
it is Helen longing for her brothers, already immortal;
the hunting owls above them live on darkness
dive into the roots of blood contending.

I listened at the edge of the anti-clockwise sea,
staring into the eyes of the serene empire
the outposts are closed, the captains all gone home,
with Taygetos, the barrier, at my back
sending down green terraces in waves.

The maqams of my brother's music
slide and return on the water, sing amanes at the sky,
and if the rocks follow along the shore to the south,
shatter and explode in the mouth of hell below Tanaeron,
then the whole world goes down with them.

Away in the dark Leuktra is awake tonight,
free city of a walking kingdom;
Ino speaks in dreams in a garden above the sea
making a pathway of living things,
so that Pephnos rises and Malovos of the shadows appears.

# Four Voices From

Telemetry, telekinesis, Telemachus, holy shit.
Tell me another one, I thought him dead but he's back;
I thought him white bones cast on black sand,
his grin from the photo I inherit—and a world of trouble.

What zinger pumped this one out, what fat mouth?
Radio Troy in the Greek Administration Zone:
father son reunion spells big trouble in Ithaka;
I might as well talk to the waves for sense.

But he's back, ready for action, ready for blood;
he sees himself in me, I'm far from fighting I said,
but then my heart fills—and this is the hard thing,
I've longed for him all my life.

He smells of smoke, drops into deep sea silence,
controls his face at sudden sounds, eyes wide.
What does it take to hollow out a man?
Black bones on white sand, his voyage, my voyage.

*

Of course he's come back, I knew he would;
they do go on the quality, like it matters:
pigs I understand—them I don't get at all,
but this one, not just crafty, he invented it.

They say the sea spat him out, he tasted tough,
spat him out in a river for a good wash.
They say a lot of things, there's a world of saying
and he's the best, it just tickles off his tongue.

He knows which side his mattress is buttered,
always has, my lord, that's why I like him.

I know I stink very bad, and I'm old but true,
it makes me young to look at him, like a boy.

I wonder if they'll sing their duet tonight,
banging her up against that bloody tree thing?
He'll get to it after the killing business,
a sort of cleaning up of screaming and smoke.

*

I didn't think he would ever return,
our lives apart unravelling, blue thread
floating on the air, a lost word gone pelagic,
but he's here, substantial, salty, like before.

His blank Trojan stare tells the story,
burning towers, lamentation turned to art;
I feared he was become no man nowhere,
and now it makes me hungry to look at him.

I was to be the woman surrounded by men,
the pack of them, soft, lascivious, grinning;
the light went out of me when he sailed off,
I poured my heart into a hole in the air.

Every night I talked and talked to an absence,
I've drawn him back, on and on I've said,
to the rise and fall of the sea—I won't have this,
come back, you must come back and speak to me.

*

Large as life Ithaka rolling under my feet,
I never thought I would get back here;
the sea never stops moving, the land now and then;
but here I am, I hold my nerve, I make it happen.

If there's an account to be given, no problem,
I'll say what I did and did not do—straight;
ships drawn up, burning towers, a woman,
if there's a pattern to this it's only visible now.

So that night I lay to sleep on the threshold,
thought of the undoing of these men, awoke
to the grinding of barley, knowledge in my bones,
the house flooded with light and the voices I know.

They stare like I've returned from the dead—well.
I look at my wife and it makes me hungry.
Dogs, see what you'll never have, never taste;
sweet slaughter of limbs, wetness and her belly.

## *Over the calm, clear shining water*

*Over the calm, clear shining water
with smiling face there came to them the longing
for a bench in a ship to scar the sea,
assaulting the divine.*

I am a straight black line, black as the cypress,
tending my relations above the harbour;
soon the ground will open up for the last one,
and I will join them in this earthy gallery.

The radio voices, the cicada telecom, sweep over me,
they mean nothing, I am a black line from the sky;
my son went to the new world, the America
—there will always be men with ambition leaving.

What I don't do won't ever be done,
the shadow of the Far Away One falls on us all;
if my son in the west thinks differently
may the earth rest lightly on him.

I listen to the secret conversation of things,
the village chorus and sea-polished stone
in the light of the pomegranate and fig,
if the bones are white then he is free.

*

Behind Yorgos' gate the sea casts white words
filling our mouths, making us say whatever we think;
all summer long we roll and shout and fall,
go down as the body of water takes a deep breath
and the world comes crashing in wave by wave.

Washed up, abandoned on all fours, shining
in the attitudes of delight, despair, of knowing nothing,
we stand with all the creatures the dark earth feeds;
where transparent altars collapse drink cool air,
the submarine foothills and rivers say welcome.

Open your arms, let Pephnos go, those figs, that life at sea;
Helen's black ship is a shadow passing over you,
the sun, a golden hand trailing in the water,
signals come, follow to the further shore;
and in its wake you swoon and spit and fall.

*

When my brothers stood in the upper world
on that rock with their hands raised,
for all my life they looked like statues.

When my brothers stood in the upper world
they promised safe passage and saved the drowned,
there was no stealth in them, just brave boys.

So when my brothers… where are they now?
they wanted nothing of me then
nor in this divinity the other side of Cythera.

Between here and Crete the murex fails
in a deep blue vertigo nations collapse,
there's no end of feeling.

They say the earth trembles still
and I dazzle the armies of the plain,
they walk on insurgent fire at noon.

What means they have for mineral wealth,
but one day the molluscs disappear
and the purple to decorate an empire is gone.

When I rise up into your minds I see
a fault runs around the world,
my brothers walked on water in mercy.

    \*

We go out into the world in the name of the first wave
breaking over the bow as it dips: blessing; baptism; ambition:
against the countries making conspiracy in their islands.

Call for the ships of Kardamyli and the fifty towns,
the earth opening its little red mouth, set back in the mind,
covered by logistics and the secret invasion of the sea.

For one moment there's no sound on the water,
the roads closed, the electricity cut, and between two bodies
light picks its way down the mountain.

We follow the head of a bird, rising and falling eastward,
sail into the heart of rage and fix our hold upon the lands
as far as the circuit of the earth for the bright pathfinder to guide us.

Inland of the shadowed coast, in the kingdom of rivers,
locked in the contracts of the world below the world
sings the geology of great wealth, starry sex and the life of ease.

Those of us who crossed the border; our seed is not.
Those who sailed into fire; our ships and goods are fallen.
Those who turned back; we don't even say the name of the place.

    \*

At the slow colouration of the world
milky dawn transposes blue
and the acacia is a net of light
thrown to catch the great iconoclast.

The wall of mountain casts off shadow,
on the opposite arms of the harbour
the chapel and Christeas's tower
stand as blown powers benign.

Where he sets his foot
the music of many drums begins,
the sound's in Thalami I think
no more than girls playing.

Leukothia, steady my sight,
let me align the arms of the harbour
and fix the point in mid blue
where all nonsense is washed away.

In that telescopic ellipse
swim all the living things,
our quick lives coming and going
in the unpeopled cities of stone.

It is light, morning light
comes walking through the village,
out of the folds of the mountain
into the folds of the sea.

# At the Centre of the World

# At the Centre of the World

this is all there is, the blue
upon blue of layered mountains
to the sea below Parnassos

Apollo and the wooded valley
at the centre of the world
all thought is thought about something

one column of smoke rises
the radio plays, I want nothing
the substance of light surrounds the hills

\*

That night snow fell softly
then morning walked on white mountains,
Melanie slept dreaming of snow
and the world turned into Spring.

\*

We found a real meadow and breathed in its smell,
right out above the sea, a meadow of tall grasses
April poppies and daisies lifted up into the sky.
Wading out on a promontory of absolute Spring
through tall grasses, blue and distant mountains,
under the eyes of the serene empire.

\*

Beyond the white church the sun depicts
the hills of the Argolid and Tiryns;
exact light, presentive and miraculous.
Seferis waking with a marble head in his hands.

# The Name Apollo

Apollo, god of words, accept my song,
let it rise like an arrow
the voice and flight of birds
[unblown and pure into the sky]

strike out into nothing,
into the [empty] air of spring
and satyrs enter, in revel, saying whatever:
I know another returns, I know

by the ivy tattooed on my arm
[the silver foil] the pigeon feather,
the flight and voice of…

You don't wrap it in mystery, in proscription
Apollo… I do the work of vision…


*


I came down from the northern forests;
furs, wax, honey and slaves:
they took me to their coastal cities,
merchants, craftsmen of the wonderful art,
from the inland sea to the ocean.

They took me for their own
to those islands I was borne;
her arms around a single tree
in a soft meadow split asunder
in the centre, miracle of light.

In my bones the white north sleeps,
each winter I return there:
they are children in the garden
making magic with stones
and hidden designs in my name.

\*


I was the chosen boy, both parents alive,
no touch of death, in the place named for me
a boy leading boys.

Dressed in laurel, dressed in light
the waking dream of spring
parades from door to door.

I took the year from the earth,
the flight and voice of vision,
made a hole in the ground speak.

# The Roadside Shrine

1

As if by arrangement four figures are spaced evenly in the foreground of the photograph; a road sign, an old man seated on a bench, an empty bench and a shrine. The road runs around the southern slopes of Parnassos. The view drops into the deep river valley, make one mistake and you die. Beyond, the mountain wall of silence rises out of the frame as you stand with your back to Delphi.

The road sign is a red circle with a red diagonal through an old fashioned car horn, more like a bugle, meaning prohibited—don't touch it. The silhouette of the old man is at rest. Hat back, walking stick propped, he looks into the valley but not, the angle of his head suggests, at the sanctuary of Athena below.

Next to the empty bench, the road side shrine is a blue display case on stilts, topped with an open fretwork cupola and cross. With glass on four sides and the mechanism on top, it could be a crane operated lucky dip machine—the tension in the claw set so that nothing of substance can be lifted. The air-blue wooden sides are weathered, the door oil stained.

You stand with your back to the sanctuary. The road is empty on a morning in Spring. Scattered with scrub and gorse, the white mountain rises.

2

The candid mountain shines
through the blue fretwork dome,
the shrine glides over the valley
a broken television on the air.

Tangled scrub surrounds the case
visible through glass on every side,
blown and spiky, a promise of life
against the dead contents exhibited.

Inside, a cameo of the patriarch
stares above a box of matches;
in the centre, a framed Christ,
casts a picture within the picture.

It looks as if sea and sky
meet in line with his shoulders,
an ouzo glass of oil on water
stands in front of him.

To the side a plastic coke bottle
ready to refuel the flame;
in all this sky and mountain
interior darkness absorbs the light.

3

In this case all we have is the succession
of deities and the memory of uncreated light,
the faded grey blue of the central figure
—a young unbearded Robert Powell cum Byzantine androgyny,
the panama halo and gaze of utter blankness
in the face of the sun as great iconoclast.

To open a window in the sky, the copy must be perfect,
as in, "When you see your brother or sister, you see God."
or, "The best icon of God is the human person."
We should praise iconodules, in particular St. John Damascene;
"…for the flower of painting makes me look,
charms my eyes as does a flowering meadow…"

The Coke bottle, fixed in plastic, does not shine,
a corruption of Samuelson's 1916 classic;
the figure dull and thickened out,
"aggressively female" as Loewy said, it sells plenty,
but in the wrong way here;
the label script full-frontal and invisible.

In the ouzo glass, viscous sunlight glows amber,
appears to ignite the oil without burning the wick;
light catches on the right of the frame
lending definition to its cheap detail:
neither effect is proof of anything
but the great Spring day rising on Parnassos.

# The Artemision Tunnel

Between the Mountains of Artemis and Lyrkio
crossing from the Argolid to Arcadia—switch on your lights—
we drive into the black tunnel, the eye of day closed.

Artemis, lady of all the animals and living things,
lead us into darkness, lead us under the mountain of your shrine.
Can we even breathe down here? We are in your hands.

If the earth drips off roots threaded through our eyes,
lady of the wild things, light-carrying Artemis,
our theme is order and the springs of Inachos rise with you.

On higher ground, surrounded by the hall of trees,
the sacrifice is without distinction, all living things
—oxen, goats and ending with small birds, thrown into the pyre.

Flocks of quail crowd the sky, as thought flies without shadow,
red hem at the knee, date palm, stag and bee, we see all of this;
against the city of unjust men she tries her bow.

The Alphios marks the boundary where her genius attends,
and after the fire in the artificial forest
I see my own family in a bright circle restored.

My parents, my children and the familiar dead stand again
at the stations of the road, westward from her hands
we climb the high, watered meadows around Asea.

The sky is empty above this temenos of orchard and arable land;
there's a garage, a collapsed house and an abandoned speed trap,
and we stand again in the great common field.

# Interview

Q. How did you get here?

At night from 36,000 feet fire
rages in the bowl of the mountains
a thunderstorm caught lightning
ignited again and again my god
I've heard the pine trees explode
on the smoking hills and cowered.


Q. What are you doing here?

When Roza Eskenazi sings
I fall under that wave.
How's it going Roza my child?
Aman, I sing and spit and swoon.
She will strip your heart
cleaner than the sea.


Q. Do you want to leave?

Leave this screen of Tamarind and Eucalyptus
surrounding our aerial garden?
The limby green layer of living things
breathes on us painted out ghosts,
by morning the white frame made empty
and the day pauses in mountain air around us.

# My Journey to Euripides

Because I knew my Euripides I survived the Latomiae,
I was of the 4,000 of the quarries;
we saw the ships go down, the sea burning
and the passes of the fertile plain blocked.

Those who did not die were sold as slaves
—somewhere to the south? I don't know;
others, like me, a few, climbed out on poetry,
the Syracusans like poetry.

But they did not see, on my inner arm,
the tattooed ivy, immortal imprint
of the immigrant stranger, lord of many names,
they did not see I was of the god of all blossoming things.

In the pit I remembered the spring when I was a boy;
in my village we observed the rites,
the year I was chosen, both parents alive,
the procession of all of us made the round.

> We walked with the year, the season
> of trees alive and the rocks moving,
> rumours took on flesh in the mountains
> and at night on the water light sang.

> I remember Hermes gave me moly
> that I might resist her,
> white flower, black root
> that I might have her.

> We ran to the high meadows
> out of the arms of the leaping god,
> the wet earth his chamber
> spring tripping in our wake.

After I had recited my way out of the pit,
I went aboard a merchant ship across the Ionian;
I swam with the low life of small fishes and other fauna,
driven by brigandage and buggery mostly.

You can spend days staring at the surface of the sea,
the gulls wingtip acrobatics, feed me feed me,
the occasional blue fin and the confused bee
—staring in fact at the glossy reflection of nothing.

It has meaning in a lost language of sound
sliding across the water and familiar harbours;
smoke drifted over the ruined villages
and starving fishermen threw dog shit at us.

By slow stages and different ships I went south;
all along the Peloponnese the same story,
a war economy with the wheels coming off
and rumours of the big crisis to end the world.

A storm wrecked us into the Messenian Gulf,
we came into the first harbour still open;
Helen's brothers stood on the rock called Pephnos
and on the water I heard the songs for Leukothia.

The village was empty of people
and I knew they would be out in the fields
at the ceremony of return and uprising,
the greater journey of the earth.

> We cooked the pots of all the seeds,
> the white poppy, barley, pulse and lentils
> but not for human food
> nor for the strengthless heads of the dead.

But for the earth people, to take down with them
for the unimagined harvest,
carried to all our weddings
when the fields rise up and each root blossoms.

We don't eat abstractions,
we burn pigs, snakes and fir cones
in a blackened hole to make the earth part,
for the unimagined harvest.

I went south in the oven of summer
around the bare finger of land for Matepan,
those days the sea filled my mind
and Laconia filled my mouth.

The submarine cave into hell was crowded,
victims of a precept blown half way across the world;
poor souls—no ghost of mallow, asphodel or orchid
flowered in the burnt dust under their feet.

And further east I arrived at Trozen
to hear the white women singing all night,
love wanders in the high meadows
in every atom of the swollen sea.

I kept Euripides before me and made for Attica;
they said Athena was lost,
all argument over and the squares empty;
incarnate city of the mind left to slow rot and irrelevance.

I remembered Pericles's speeches,
their perfect syntax cut from marble
singing over our heads in the market place,
we repeat them even as we fall.

Those monuments of the air,
made from what is sweet and what is terrible,
drove us on to meet what came
—by then I'd had my fill of both.

Later, when Spartans planned to raze the lot,
with Euripides silent in final exile,
one voice rose to sing his words
and no hand was lifted against Athena.

Well, my soul was pastured there too;
unscorched by invasion, in the glories of knowledge,
my journey became a perfect map of itself
and I walked in two worlds with each step.

I had been north through the Vale of Tempi,
mountains piled up, wall upon wall of snow
polished by the sun, serrating the world,
the passes gone over to a sort of blindness.

Did everything turn to a whiteness in the end?
Even the turquoise sea in a white rage
lifted each wave into a booming nothing
and the levelled plain was not the floor of heaven.

I found him at the court in Macedon,
I was not the first to make the journey;
in the bowl of the mountains, at the end of reason
the great mind near empty.

He looked like bones collapsed, half blind,
fit for the dogs or whatever ceremony was there;
his breath like a bird passing
made one note in the frozen sky.

I am Alexiares of the Latomiae,
I stood where Athens over reached itself
and landed in a hole, 4,000 at my shoulder;
I stand opposed, above ground in the air.

I repeated each word, each strophe
lifting me out of the pit,
out of the dumb quarry into the light;
and the seas and islands echoed him.

    I am Dionysus, lord of many names,
    of the bull, the snake, the lion
    mixing all forms of life;
    I glide over the pit.

    The city is drowned in ivy,
    I will give you what you want
    and the streets and precincts catch light.
    Is it dawn rising, my fresh girl?

    I am Dionysus, I call in my own
    from the fields of Lydia and Phrygia;
    when the cup is empty, even to the shadow,
    I am manifest, the empire of confidence.

# From Alexiares' Notebooks

Three village children walked into the courtyard last night,
they stood in a line singing and ringing triangles
—may St. Basil bless you, a long life on your house;
this was for new year's eve and a reward of sweets.

The boy Apollo, both parents alive, would lead the children
in our procession of the spring, they would strike the door and sing
—all time is blossoming, green stick, dry stick, young shoot sprout,
strike the door and anyone in the path of the risen year.

I heard triangles ringing across the whole country,
an Orthodox suite for a thousand manic bell towers;
may there be a long life for your house the air chimes,
teach us your alphabet St. Basil, the voices rising call.

*

At night on the corner of the post office
Hermes of the underworld takes flight,
his jet steam curls and sense of purpose
alights on the thin faced Albanian boys.

The 15 Euros a day labourers smoke and commune,
they ride in the back of early morning pick-ups
straight backed carrying a remittance economy,
experts at shaping stone for traditional houses.

Vagelis told us, in Albania, once ago it was ok,
I had a home by the sea, a big house;
the rich countries suck in the poor across the world,
15 Euros would be for something skilled, like tiling.

The boys saunter in this easy darkness
and the village kids play slow-mo football,

a balloon floating over the collective heads;
the whole scene swims in sweet air like honey.

*

Fat leaved ivy pours over the broken wall
down the sides of the Taygetos
splitting the rocks of the terraces.

I stuck my head inside the box of spring,
sweet song of flowers, frogs and birds
rising up from the green in one breath.

The day comes calling out of the blue,
on the salt pans and rock pools
the sea drops a whole synod of little gods.

*

What did Ovid do all day,
smell the harbour, count his syllables,
see the black sea light soak the wall
mapping the edge of utter darkness
and curse the frost on the face of Augustus?

I pile the white stones in the corners
for their click, the beautiful painted bodies
of the men and women who take their shapes
from the shapes of the olive groves, smoke rising
over the blue hills of the earth turning.

I follow Europa and her bull in the wet meadow,
they vanished in the spray zone's magnetic air
beaded with every singing world;
she holds on, mouth open, I don't know,
his smile lights up another country.

*

I've not written a word to you for weeks;
the Spring weather is gentle, the air like balm
has made my mind candid and I can't bear to be inside.

So I sleep and eat and fuck like a little god,
the sea shush shushing us land children
out along the shore running to the end of the world.

The village wakes to dog-barking dawn and
all the birds practise their scales in Greek,
I can feel the earth tilting into first light.

I dreamt the music of how the night comes
in the lemon groves and orange groves of the Argolid
and walked the rising hills to the village of lights

Towards a mask of gold, behind which there's no darkness,
only the dreaming air sweet as mountain honey;
here it comes, here comes the night, the Beautiful Door opening.

*

I have not told you enough about last night in the Albanian taverna
where the wine is deep and takes you down with it;
these boys in their red nylon jumpers and football shirts
—Sweden 1986, the poorest of the poor of Europe, Jesus
their ring tones and house building for English and Germans;
in this absurd channel of the world market a Chinese girl
walking from village to village, now goes table to table
not selling plastic toys and watches to displaced peasants;
you almost imagine a country they've left at home.

They are gentle in their manners under the American film,
under the presence of men like Alec Baldwin actors;
heavy on the common air the atomized cash circulates
around the table where Ovid stares, writing letters Roma/Amor,
save me Augustus from these fucking barbarians;

—next time you come and dance in Albania;
the big screen blonde in a blonde bikini in blonde America
snaps the boy's eyes like magnets to attention,
then they return to their beer and smoke and courtesies.

Ritsos tips his head to the glide and wail of the clarino,
his hands hold that face in the mountain village,
rearranging the white stones of his risen nation;
an archipelago of men and women reach across the Aegean.
Look Ritsos, off in the corner, the wrecked sailor stands,
Ithaka the birthmark in the crook of his left arm;
he wants to write the final chapter, straight as an arrow;
and then we can scatter the bloody pages of the kanun
in the mouth of the harbour to feed the silver fishes.

—And next time you dance the deep wine in Albania,
the clarino rising over any mountains and valles we have to hand,
its slide and figuration describes what land this is Illyria lady
and I am letting the little iambs out into the fields;
we do a kaba, berati say, and then step it up koftos for a wedding,
—I thought it was from Epirus, yes yes is all the same music;
I am letting the little riot, wave the flaming napkin, then step
over the border, see, the generations in my feet, step
the frontiers disappearing dance, and step step.

*

Beyond all of this with morning just risen
a rumour in the mountain villages,
the white horse runs from his shadow.

Nostrils sharp as fluted marble,
the vaporous sun streams from his flanks,
muscles flicker in one wave.

Pulse beating on the chambered earth,
the white horse in the high meadow
runs over terraces of light.

# Alexiares in Exile

1

After the last journey I began another,
though not exactly Ithaka, despite Cavafy;
I opened my instructions in a different country,
sailing blind in the sea lanes of Morse code.

The sun strikes the tower, a massive gnomon;
time is nothing here, over and out
the land running south in blue layers,
the villagers call it a promontory of song.

It rises as a sort of Egypt of now and then,
a land bridge of animals and plants
for Martin Bernal to dance across
so that imports follow in strict measure.

An early naturalism, alive and immediate,
the African Blue Lily or Agapanthus,
your name in a burning circle on the ground:
work it out by next dispatch.

2

Again last night the sun died red into the sea,
this is hardly news I know but the sky caps the black
and my mind is elsewhere over the singing water;
engine of the world, ace of ambition, floored me.

Thalassa Mavri they sing, well they might—Greeks;
I am in exile between textual variants,
head down in darkness dancing out such poems
would make the emperor of goats weep.

Here I barely stick to the rim of the world,
a brown river and a thin wall against the hoards,
they come screaming off the frigid steppes;
it is a strange form of exegesis I suffer.

On the sea's bend sinister stands the bridgehead,
I hide behind the wall, holding a stick, shaking;
Athena—come, love me again, give me one more chance,
not this brightness pissed into a marsh under a black sky.


3

What am I doing here? How do I know?
I was sent out into this condition
with no secret gate east or west,
this is Tomis, Samos, London transit camp.

My body's made invisible to me,
a shape inside a shape of nothingness;
I float on my neighbour's language,
it leaves me undisturbed, untroubled.

They seem well disposed and incomprehensible;
the other morning they were up early,
before the sea had taken its colour
and went off singing in the woods.

Later, bread appeared on my window ledge,
it was cinnamon bread, I ate if for breakfast;
I am not speaking truth to power,
I watch the sparrows peck about the broken wall.

4

At night the sea piles up its sound,
no one will sail against this wall of water
and the mind falters, sliding off the wind
over the boats abandoned in the harbour.

Smoke thickens and songs by Xylouris go round,
—at one time all these songs were banned;
the little red tanks of the eager insurgents
arrive in waves, their eyes like heavenly spheres.

Will we survive the brilliant strategy?
security calculated in ships which sink;
they say the logos was constant in Athens,
all aliens thick-tongued barbarians: what nerve.

I held the idea of an island suspended
in the deep sea between three continents;
and this song can make you drunk,
just listen and you will be big time intoxicated.


5

When I walk through the streets of mud,
between the wooden palisades and nephos,
garish billboards cover the sky
sending the dumb dumb message mainstream.

I walk out of their dream, the war on abstract nouns,
and see we have fallen into the hands of thieves,
the barbarians who need barbarians
to make the bloody business spin.

After the blast I witnessed illumination;
the family photographs tattered but untouched,
poor souls they flew away at last
but nothing will replace the absence of your face.

A massive darkness sits on my shoulder,
I float in the broken signal of the short-wave;
all night the black sea spits out our first language
and the streets falter in earthy tracts.


6

I found co-ordinates to prehistoric creatures
lying frozen in rock pools, the first cuneiform;
a music like letters in polished scales
lifting up from the earth every spring.

I found the uncovered mosaic on the cape,
a ditch, a temple, a chapel and god
the model worked—but if the ground gives way
no bloody aroko of the Rebus tribe will save you.

Nor does the meaning of the sky vary
—trail of stars, boom: trail of stars, stop:
those who sent me don't see the indifference,
how perfect syntax dismantled Ilium.

And god the beautiful trees of the mountain
in banks and hills go rising up,
like promised countries around the world
the beautiful trees opened their arms.

7

Rain has released the smell of wild garlic
and splashed blue cyclamen across the path;
mosaic of light on the insect-laden air
bears the unfinished music of the small gods passing.

In darkness the outboard of the fishing boat
binds the edge of a black sea blanket
and marine white noise floods the frontiers of the world,
the work songs of the faithful at the final catch.

In these lost villages of the terraced mountains
the most complex ladders to the stars
were made by Ottoman musicians,
masters of the clarino, the sisters of amanes.

And all night I hear them shape from the air
the heavenly body of our starry queen,
they open a door in the endless sky
with Apollo's bees dancing attendance.


8

The sun strikes the tower, a massive gnomon,
time is nothing here, over and out;
on the collapsed ramparts of the golden west
they have lost the power of naming.

What am I doing here? I don't know.
My neighbours sing—the black wall of the far one
leans over us closely tonight—I would not surrender
one moment of happiness to explain this to you.

It looks like Apollo, the whole singing world,
laid out across the grey slab,
but there's no end of feeling in the sky
and the lights of home are like poured honey.

The wind is looking to blow the village flat
and the sea boils in a white rage at the harbour wall,
a child in a wedding dress over her jeans and trainers
flits from door to door like a bird.

# Myriorama

# Sea Table

From this wooden ramp
the total blue spectrum
lifts the sky westward,
the wave cache ascatter
reshaping the Neolithic deal
and Mycenaean rethink.

My table at the window
sets off into the gulf,
one leg tilts, a saucepan ring
embellished in soft pine,
cast off into white particles
launched from this ramp.

*

Change came hand to hand
along new exchange routes
dreaming a map of desire
goods and beliefs unwrapped.

Copper tin gold silver
amber marble lapis lazuli
oils perfumes wines we want
trained horses and wives.

Change came from across the sea
on a boat men with different hair
their words on the water
their eyes sea-green asking.

*

I can't get over the shape of your
mouth the upward promise open
around the words into which I fall.

*

(this table used to belong to
John Gould Oxford classicist
he sat at his table and
drilled eloquent into the past)

*

Orion rises over my gate
rests his right foot on the tower
there's movement in the sea tonight
but no fireflies flicker in the harbour
no thoughts ignite the world.

Only the lit graves of Easter
keep the dead with us don't
let them go into the falling darkness
that's your own life you see memory
a stream of cold air in the riverbed.

*

Renegade, excommunicant
Platonist, revolutionary
inventor of the Renaissance
beloved of the Medici
Gemistos / Plethon
draws up to my table
and looks at the sea.

*

Dear Cosimo, here's the point:
to set things right in their kind
is not a trick, a new weapon or CDO;
the end, you see, is different.

When I was young I walked the shore,
saw heretics flung in the glassy sea,
their arms and legs broken—swim, swim;
true faith gasped at every breath.

I'm at my lookout point,
the plain rolls out to Sparta
the future at my back westward,
further even than Rome.

The ocean of thy goodness,
thy boundless mercy to man;
the flow of ideas turns
and is fatal, yes we have no.

\*

Recordings of the sea from
several locations in Messenia,
from behind the tower
in bright April swimming.

In the harbour at night
wind and waves funnel music
all night the sea
working on its language.

Constant shingle channels in
from the left an orderly sentence
though the bay, the stones chorus
sounds submerged boustrophedon.

And a bird a finch I think
above the path back from the sea
lyric rising and falling
Spring visiting the world

On wings of digital mimesis
the god of the air releases
modulated below the red zone
his new ancient song with a bullet.

    *

Mystras might rise and fall
the Ottoman tide turn but shit
my foot is riddled with something.

The fingers on my right hand
white and cold at the tips but
still there's an argument to make.

And another winter comes sluicing
through the Monemvasia gate to wash
away Aristotle and repaint the gods.

All night I dreamt I heard the sea,
the voice of the sea
in the blue morning made visible.

What is the light doing to the layered
slopes of the mountain and the cypress
climbing out of the dark folds?

Something I cannot name
calls—Byzantium Byzantium
by morning visible for miles on miles.

Plethon meaning plenty, abundant
a furnace lit in Anatolia, Plethon pitched
between Sparta and a piss-yellow dawn.

Malatesta retrieved his bones
carted off to adorn Rimini and
invent the west's Renaissance.

Ships sink and without trade—nothing;
without the border guards' songs—nothing:
calculate the fallout of the Fourth Crusade.

*

Lady of the Way, Hodeghetrio
the inner knowledge
                                  and the outer
show us the way
                                  restore the city.

Today we have no petrol,
tomorrow we waste a crop of peaches;
roads blocked, post office gone, today
we have no times around the corner.

And then my neighbour called Helen
called, to speak about the troubles;
and it was a Greek morning for talk
and the history was hardly random.

*

A poor man running by the table,
his hand takes the food, the light
shines through him, oracular.

The throne of dread necessity occupied
by beasts, the voice of fire speaks
in every square where reason lost.

Antiquities taken to order, clay figures
lamps, vases, a Mycenaean seal ring
a horse long legged spare and free.

The running man loose limbed
running the force field bronze,
the light shines through him.

*

Waves break along the shore
packing crates, moulded polystyrene,
a red cap without a head.
Haul up.

Off that cape the deepest water,
invisible forest of blind depth
of bioluminescent forms.
Haul up.

Where Europa rides half sublime,
open eyed with her darling bull
sparkling little gods and goddesses.
Haul up.

Egyptians and the boys of
fifty towns, float open mouthed
under a glassy shine.
Haul up.

*

Boss, help me boss    iPad
see is good    stolen good
not Mafia  look in the box
not Mafia  sure iPad iPhone.

Look I give you both  help me
my family  both €250  for my family
look I give you  you take home
boss, help me boss    iPad.

In Monistraki, the desperate
a man in a suit of Ikea bags
woven blue underwater shuffle
another covered in sump oil.

A third led by a toy dog stares
the running man flickers by
the newly immiserated
in procession under the Parthenon.

\*

From this wooden ramp today
the sea like blue steel shines
a line of light on the edge of
morning in 3D at the harbour
the many sounds of the waves
water falling drawn back into
a temporary white noise of
the song of pebbles piling
up in every room of the house
making a mosaic of the air.

\*

Radio Byblos on air
sang the Anne Carson summer
Big Money fails to pay
alphabet soup for the poor.

The starting point is
ordinary language and this
a claim from Gemistos
yes we have no bananas.

The water is deep
and we can drown
by repute it's crowded
all us men and women.

So all that summer
my neighbours were
the hummingbird moth
and the carpenter bee.

Boats out of the water
the empty harbour receives
bougainvillea wedding
paper fleet sails the deep.

Swirling through the mountain
light's gone behind the sky
we cut the eucalyptus, the pine
tuned the wind for winter.

Last square of sunlight
warmed my feet, a day
won from the season
the sea loading its gun.

So all that summer
my neighbours were
the hummingbird moth
and the carpenter bee.

*

Then set said table to breakers
four legs up, rigged a sail, held on,
paddled like mad, farewell
Koroni, Methoni, golden Venice.

There were days of no wind,
bands of darker blue proved false;
days under a magnifying glass
held every sound where it began.

Set course for the Cape
to periploi the mouth of hell,
What dance is that? Against time
wave after wave, into the Aegean.

White engine of thought
brought to the table;
of marble, of obsidian
the first figures stand.

# Three Monologues

## LEUKOTHIA

I am Leukothia, goddess of calm waters,
from the depths I watch the chambers of the sea;
I am companion to Poseidon,
call me mistress of good voyaging.

In my mortal story I was Ino,
daughter of Cadmus, lover then wife of Athamas,
sister of Semele the mother of Dionysus;
my other sister dismembered the fool Pentheus.

I saved the boy god, dressed the darling as a girl;
Hera drove me to madness and death for it and
my perfect dive into those arms,
in that world I breathe water.

Now I speak truth in dreams from the well,
the dark well-house of Thalami;
whatever the villagers ask is revealed,
a wet hole in the earth speaking.

In the spring they carry me out to their fields;
they ripple and wave for me,
men tightening sinews in my name;
they honour me with their blood and fucking.

They say of me, they say of me
but who is speaking, do you think,
out of the well's dark mouth?
Even their dreams echo my voice.

But I long for the earth, the waving corn,
the boy god of my village standing up;
then in one moment the wave rises
turning limbs in vaulted light.

*

So I do what I can to save them,
they come from Albania, Iraq, India;
they walk, hide in containers and small boats.
I save them if I can, thinking of the voyage;
they come from Romania, Afghanistan, Iran;
from darkness to darkness, I lift them up.

They are not the first to journey this way,
I remember the Pelasgian and the Minyan,
and the great flood to the west, the new America;
the endless weeping at doors and harbours,
enough to make starvation seem a luxury;
I remember Europa and the white turbine.

Think about what they want to escape,
to face danger and at best indifference;
show me Kurdistan on a map,
show me the remittance economies of faith;
he is not my brother, she is not my sister,
from darkness to darkness I lift them up.

*

I am Leukothia, opening my arms to you,
the wave rises, turning limbs in vaulted light,
I hold you in my hands one moment
magnified before the white crash.

## The Ingliss Touriste Patient

What do you mean too late? Is he in danger?

And I was afraid and thought I would die,
lifting off the table, only the ceiling above me
and the vertiginous air for your voice Melanie.
—Yesterday you should bring him, you must
be like sleep now, you must go to the hospital.

Next to Yorta, unconscious—ella Yorta, ella ella,
wake up wake up my daughter, my child;
Yorta—Aorta—Iota not caring one jot,
there's something wrong with a letter,
a letter is unconscious, a letter is Maria's daughter
next to Aorta, mine, something is wrong with the invisible.

Stand up.
Close your eyes.
Stand feet together.
You have the hurt problem.

I was there and not there,
under the great weight of the water
with the silver jackals and companions of the sea
suspended by a taste for the shape they once had;
diamonds of light dance over them,
they sit in a circle shining and grin,
—look at me, look at these anchors, look at these roots,
—down here the mind is overcome.

And I was there and not there,
wheeled off to brain scan land.
Where is my wife? Will I come back here? Where is she please?
Που είναι η γυναίκα μου; Θα έρθω πάλι εδώ; Σας παρακαλώ πείτε μου που είναι;
She's with the gypsies from the big camp
sliding along the corridors, riding hips,

I was back in the cardboard town by the airport,
—where do they come from?
—from here, they come from here.
Sliding along the dark corridors,
her hand holding up the baby's head to light the world.

Gracious Maria found us cold water;
she sat by her daughter all night,
drowsy Yorta recovering, Yorta the beautiful,
and Melanie thanked her for her help,
—oh but we are all people, yes.

I was there and not there:
Pound in the olive grove raging,
a ghost white man waving a broken branch
in the perfect climate for the human nervous system;
the olive tree blown green and white and
the air like a lens for the Earth given a fair chance;
Pound went down to the ship, Europa, the wreckage,
raging, raging at the innocent ants of my harbour,
its arms open to the various world.

I was there and not there with my wife and my mother;
we stared at a small television at our feet, the size of a dark footlight;
it was the emergency services concert,
—firemen, bare-chested, singing Bohemian Rhapsody,
which was not to my taste;
we stood around the dark hole at our feet,
companionable and variously entertained.

My head was away and singing:
an' war'ly cares an' war'ly men/May a' gae tapsalteerie, O
my girls wait by the sea, longing for the waves,
green grow the rashes, O standing up so straight.

My head was away and singing:
all night I saw with my eyes closed

squares of blue black landscape,
thinking my eyes were open,
villages and tracks, cisterns, temples, bus lanes and hospitals;
a series of design features made for civilisation
before it was named; and talking and water channels,
a mythology rising at every turn, local, particular and useful.
At last with my eyes open in the new day,
surprised not to see the landscapes imprinted on the world,
checking again and again, I was ready.

From Cambos, the air heavy with eucalyptus rolled over the car,
sweet pine and burnt dust off Taygetus drenched the road
and through Kardymyli jasmine in waves fell upon us;
so you kept driving and I lay down and the full moon
made its path across the water and I was there.

## Pytheas

I am Pytheas of Massalia,
I sit and watch and drink.

When I speak I am not believed,
I will die on this dockside in the sun.

I watch the ships sail away and return,
captive in thought circumscribed by Strabo.

\*

I sailed into a greater knowledge,
driven by a curiosity stronger than any trade wind;
I saw all the things and places I tell you.
I did not follow a picture of the world,
whether from Miletus or Egypt: I looked,
I saw the invisible Isle of the Pritanni.

I talked and bartered my way across Armorica
to the sea at the supposed edge of the world;
the trade in knowledge was local,
what Agde knew of Carcasso and Carcasso of Gironde;
I joined each link with my own hands,
then took ship from Ushant to the tin islands.

I cast my words like rope to secure the boat,
pulled into harbours for which you had no names;
we stuffed our boxes with gold and silver coins,
perfume, coloured glass and exotic trinkets.
We were hungry for tin, the magical alloy,
to run the arms race against Carthage.

Has the world changed much at all? I doubt it.
Are there still elites and prestige goods?
Consider who wants you not to find out for yourself,
add it up, exchange outside theogeny;
for immediate and dangerous knowledge
I swapped gifts with strangers and stepped ashore.

The great ocean put the chill in my bones,
I stood on the promontory called Belerion
bright and shining one, after 95 nautical miles;
this single fact dismantles your geography.
I crossed the land bridge to their market,
saw the Pretanni work the tin in clever ways.

The painted ones called it Albion,
Apollo flies at the back of their sun;
island by island and further inland by foot,
the flight paths, alignments, circles of stone,
rectangular fields and riches buried for gods;
after 95 nautical miles I measured it.

\*

I wait in this room over the drink shop,
Winter wraps a cloak around the harbour.

Water flops against the empty quay
and light in waves spreads across my ceiling.

My dry bones whisper the great ocean,
open the box, a knucklebone of tin.

# Myriorama

By the houses of the living
and the houses of the dead
congregation of flames burn.

A door opened in the ground
releases the great blackness,
first light unfurled the sky.

Keeper of the chambered sea,
they say that in the sea…
the story is widespread.

Details vary along the coast,
but the baby Ino, was a god?
—out of a box from the sea.

*

Under the bronze mountains spring walks,
girls follow in translation
one moment in the garden tracing Lusieri.

Blinds make bars across the page,
errant note? No, I remember the bliss
of the lines, my eyes opening on them.

Byron's estates in Eng-a-land
annexed to the big idea,
[exeunt the peasantry through every possible landscape]

I cast the cards of the myriorama
for musing swains and lacustrine vistas,
traffic jams and haunted bedrooms.

Turner asking Elgin for £400 p.a.
—I have been obliged to be a little barbarous—
and the Cretan fish eating all Lusieri's pictures.

Ten men line up to shoot Judas for Easter,
Nicolo dancing on the ruins of empire,
Nicolo dancing on broken stones and harbours.

Yannis Ritsos is free.

*

As we came out of the mountains
the moment not day or night,
music surrounded us.

Out of the silence of the gorge
through walls of rock and air,
we walked in a tunnel of sound.

Long-song synthesised unearthly,
swirl of sea and Taygetos
shatters into goat bells.

Reforms into music of the passes,
random harmonics, goat stink
rises up to us earth song replete.

*

This is Radio Free Byron on the short wave
broadcasting to the English shires: wake up.
We urge war against the west, against Fletcher;
the Maniots are the men for me, they will do the deed.

Wake up you boys and girls, you sneak careerists,
forget the English Bores co-option of Ashbery,

the discontinuous prose continues;
this is the big poem of right belief—immaculate

That black speck veering across your sky space
above the town where you live,
riding cold fronts off the map,
homing in, set at zero, is your death

With this magnifying glass in both hands
I burn sunspots on the calendar,
burn for canonic, burn for garland on your head,
so each day comes up fresh with a hole in it.

\*


Running the high meadows
day and night in the skin of a lynx
the bloody meniscus sticks.

Swallows roll in mountain air,
pop music, something emotional, defiant,
reaches into the same blue quarter.

Yannis Ritsos is free.

## Ambelakia

All afternoon the birds of Ambelakia sing
and the air is the shape of itself
rising in one breath to Olympus and Ossa;
that light should have substance and sound.

The Common Company of Ambelakia founded 1778,
founded on madder, sheep blood and method,
the red dyed cotton of the first co-operative.
"We have decided to renew our company,
spreading a table for all... in the dress of communication..."

Schools   Libraries   Hospitals   Mansions   Welfare

In 1811 Ali Pasha, sociopath and maverick,
admirer of Byron's ears, raided the village.
By 1820, with the rise of Manchester as king,
the fall of the Bank of Vienna and the war of greater powers,
the beneficent society collapsed.

Remember the Common Company of Ambelakia,
the first industrial co-operative.
Remember schools; libraries; hospitals; mansions; welfare.

\*

The painted ceilings and walls of the houses
depicted real and imagined cities,
young girls gazed down from balconies
and the world abounded with birds and flowers,
as the high meadows with aconite, anemone and cyclamen.

The full moon is high tonight,
the spring sky milky with stars;
other villages cast like sparks
shine out across the valleys.

# The Objects Were Not Paid For or Got for a Fixed Price (Elgin)

As they lowered the last metope marble rain fell on their faces,
"Telos." The Disdar stepped into history and with him the five       (Clarke)
girls crying for their sister, the ravished one, ready for shipment
in the lower town, filling the air with lamentations.                (Douglas)

The events dictate a mythology of fact and we wait for the girl
to return in Spring. "Milor explored in the bowels of the earth to
dig them up." Milor stole gods to that coast of no return, to the    (Benizelos)
shadow world below this light; the triumph of Eng-a-lish classicism. (Byron)

Milor ripped the Panathenaic frieze from the walls of the cella
where the goddess dwelt. It is the procession of all her people
translated into stone and she the city incarnate. "To realise its
meaning we must always think it back into its place."                (Harrison)

Of the money Elgin received half repaid to the government in debt;
the objects thus an integral part of the British Museum collection.  (Smith)

## *Early morning frost*

Early morning frost this morning,
white ghost packing blue fields away,
turning from night, these counties
run to the capital, pale horse racing.

Thinking your dark body asleep in my hands,
thinking big sun raging
from a slab of marble sea,
anaesthetised by Duveen out of Elgin.

But to wake on Ossa in spring,
at each step a grove, a secret stream,
the air rings under an endless sky
waiting for a figure to appear.

In delight a door opens in the air,
we see the whole of Thessaly rising.

# Disclaimer: ~~Byron Never Went to Ambelakia~~

"I saw before me in the vivid occupation of the people of that place a living notion of the world made good, a species of heresy, a society unfallen— just suppose this were known in England—the very thing I had traversed the theatre of war to find, here…"

He saw the Common Company of Ambelakia working,
the houses, the schools, the three hundred workshops,
he saw Shelley plain and the technology of genius.

As polyphonic bird song filled the air
he saw Ali Pasha's troops rise out of the Vale of Tempi,
indifferent men climbing the foothills of Ossa.

To exact murder, taxes, arbitrary arrest,
invisible powers of empire on their backs,
he saw the same beset the Nottingham weavers.

He saw the enormous condescension of posterity
rise up and he retreated into the house of George Mavros,
all thought and poise gone.

Milord knocked clean off his box.

# From the Harbour

We spring out of the box of winter,
that curling cloud, a letter—Chalcolithic,
that girl leaning towards you,
that shadow in your cup—is from my hand.

I wait at the door to your house, ivy tattooing the wall,
spurge blooms on the hill behind me;
I swept down from Thrace and the narrow pass
from blueprint villages in Anatolia to this warm water port.

Where is my sister now?
the light in slices shot through your thinking dark,
and the sky cracking over the whole world.
My sister?—trumpets calling from the water.

I swept down, my birds in random green go mad,
on to this landing strip between mountain and sea,
into this natural amphitheatre
I set my foot for riot to follow.

The ground returns my tread, the chambered earth, and she steps ashore.

*

I found a plastic bull on the beach,
toy Zeus fronting the waves erect
with bleached hide and shrivelled horn
—if he grins girls, you're over his back
crashing towards a bed of luxury, where it all begins.

He has the look of you about him Byron,
the set of his head and lordly gaze,
though I forget we are both dead
I think you would like him,
he bellows sweet amphionic odes.

Let's walk him along the cape,
spring begins again with his snort;
we danced all our lives to his delicate step,
to the beat of his blood, even now
as old as we are, descending in shadows.

Yours, Shiloh

        \*


Those stories, those songs were television to us
except alive on air they wrapped us in their signal,
except that we ran it and it was real
in the grain of the wave as we cleared the harbour.

So, like birds in the wilderness, we are its variations,
making the picture atomised, the republic of light,
and the sea shaping a tunnel of sound
as long and slow as summer around the western shore.

        \*


After his victory at Actium Octavius founded Nicopolis,
a blighted shithole befitting his political soul:
call him Blair, Bush, Sharron or Milosevich,
those who are wired to the world, who cannot set ambition aside.

Of Antony an old man said, he was glued to her,
a lover's soul lives in the body of his mistress
and she set sail for the Peloponnesus;
off Taenarus her women reunited them.

They spoke and afterwards did sup and lie together;
across the dark calm of the sea Antony said,
—we are keeping company with famous ghosts,
Helen and Paris sailed this way to their final sortie.

Let's glide to the cave below the headland
and paddle in the mouth of hell, hand in hand
we'll walk the streets of our burning city
and gather the asphodel of our sweet defeat.

*

Stack the myriorama vertically,
each card suspended apart
a spatial landscape made temporal,
olive tree blown white in the wind.

Seeds, insects crowd the air,
oil from the boatyard bleeds into concrete,
at night Kurds come ashore
we turn them round if we can.

The walls flake into the sea,
palimpsest, underwriter
of this harbour between worlds
opening its broken arms.

# Byron's Karagiozis

This lake and town of Byron's escape
appears as fresh as a boy's face;
milord's playthings arrayed across the plain,
the shoreline stepping in and out of the ever living past.

The Pasha scans the mountain paths for rebels
rising to the blue of Ottoman heaven,
saunters along the landing strip of the unaligned
—my palace, my lands of blood, my lord—welcome.

We dropped out of thin air over the Pindhus,
a door opened became a flood of light;
landing gear scarring the face reflected
the water full of boats and sacked women.

This the first Albanian song of Lordy Viron,
the second a lamentation of unrequited love;
the clarinos sob sob, the real men howl
—ah your pink ears, their coral portal and lightshine.

*

Scene 1

Enter Spiridion Foresti, British Consul, dancing with the Governor of Malta, cloaked in smiles—'We can send young Byron to traverse the province, let him bind the Pasha by his vices to our cause, and just think how well it will be received—an Albanian front against Napoleon.'

'Does the young lord have to know? Reputation says he's of the same kind, he can be our Karagiozis, with a big fat cock to catch the devil.' A paper boat bobs across the screen, the Spider, British warship, flags flying, and off goes Byron to Prevesa, dumb little thing in a puppet show.

*

The music is different village to village,
in my village Konitsa, it is lighter, other places
sadder—like the stone we build black or white,
the stone is just for that village, the right stone.

But the songs, most songs, all over about the same,
being away, not home, songs of away, to say exile,
as they play for you, you know Saturday, off work,
the longing of Albania or another Greece or Germania.

*

Eleftheria showed us the painted Ottoman door
taken from the dump, under the blackened surface
a blue green meadow of flowers and birds interwoven
flooding a lattice of apricots and pinks.

Idealised peony or rose, an eternal spring at the centre
the habitation of songbirds, rescued from the tip,
—we keep it here, not in our rooms, so all can see
and the colours of the house are taken from it.

*

From the capital of the East
two experimental cantos,
the minarets of Tepelene like meteorites
—who now shall lead the scattered children forth?

Journey made difficult by Ramadan and rain
nine hours lost in the storm at Zitza,
we lit fires, fired guns to find the party;
Byron, cloaked to his eyes, under a rock, content.

Remembered lowering coast and the name—Missolonghi,
dark mind on darker waters held silent;
Wahhabi's rebel brood, their pious spoil
a path of blood running to the west.

At Ioannina the houses and domes
glitter through gardens of lemon and orange trees,
the lake spreads itself from the cypress grove
making a track into a land of no fixed boundaries.

*

Scene 2

At the Karagiozis staged for Ramadan, Hobhouse and Byron agog;
on the other side of the art of the theatre of shadows
Captain Leake unloads guns and ammunition,
Ali Pasha enters, raises his eyebrows and pats the ordnance.

Byron skips on in Albanian finery, begins a letter—My Dear Mother,
he reveals to the audience an enormous penis strung from his neck;
straining, he soliloquises and beats the beast, rolling across the floor,
admiring his guest's performance, eyes alight, the Pasha approaches.

*

The stone villages rise and fall
as if abandoned on rolling Zagori,
we saw photographs of children
on the walls of all the tavernas.

Formal, dressed in white
for a festival in the platea,
rows and rows of children
from fifty years ago.

*

You must be quiet crossing the bridge,
stop the music, dismount and step softly.

Don't let the one sacrificed below
catch us at our wedding in this upper world.

If she hears the music she'll join the party,
the bridge collapse and we'll never cross over.

       *

Scene 3

A large room paved with marble, a fountain playing at the centre, men lounge and suck sherbet; then to a rough fanfare painted boys in spinning circles sing 'Oh your curling hair and small ears.'—Ali, ornate craft borne aloft by many hands, responds profundo, 'You must think of me as a father, a father, a father.'

As the tide of seduction rises with pretty animals, sweetmeats and aerial Ali, the devil descends and affixes the monster penis to the image of every future lover, mistress, wife and sister of the alarmed poet: Byron darkens and grits his teeth, smoke form his burnt journals obscures the scene.

      *

Streets dark all day, damp
tip tap from the dance school,
houses slumped in glutinous air
nothing for it but drown in the lake.

I am sick of vice, tried all its varieties,
it's time to leave off wine and carnal company
and betake myself to politics and decorum;
—a vast mountain that little word.

Then from the bazaar a wedding party dances,
her hat of gold coins, her face painted red and white,
the men singing—Erotica Erotica, a sweet song for ladies
echoes off the whole world, the girl in coins glinting.

Looking at you what language is left?

The passes we travelled have left a river running in my heart.

The dragomen were silent crossing the bridges.

In that small bay Antony lost the world.

*

The Albanian girls circle the square
on bikes borrowed from the Ingalish,
—thank you, thank you, we bring back,
silver spokes turning spindly legs push.

They circle under the tower's long shadow
and the day darkens for time to stop,
the mountains come falling down falling down
and the world walks away on terraced light.

*

Scene 4

On this side of the art of the theatre of shadows
Ali Pasha is beheaded by his Ottoman masters in 1822,
the blue and white flags of a new nation flood the land
and Byron, poster boy in exile, would lead the children forth.

*

By morning we woke in the bowl of mountains,
snowbound peaks shining up the sky chemicals
of the big fat day on its feet and shouting.

The clarino rising wails—what word, what root will break
the rock wolves in rounds, heads back sing, pelts spark
black Zagori night unveils the first light of another country.

## Apokriatika

Driving across to the Mani this February we broke the journey in Corinth. Slept the night in a stone cold room in the Hotel Shadow and ate at the taverna used by the villagers for a night out. We thought nothing of the children dressed in Pierrot costumes and Disney. Later I thought I saw a goat faced man outside the door in pitch darkness wearing a white veil, I thought his friend was wearing a Dolly Parton-style wig.

Next morning we drove on and saw big red and green kites on sale everywhere. Men standing and talking at the *kafeneio* were dressed in ball gowns and wigs. Well, village life we thought, you make your own entertainment. We found out the next day it was carnival—Apokriatika, the last weekend before Clean Monday of only fish and vegetables, but for now pre-lenten celebrations held sway. I remembered the carnival songs; cocks and cunts dancing around fruit trees, young boys being taken in hand by aunty at the mill and black straw faced devils chasing through the streets.

\*

From the Hotel Shadow on the edge of spring
under the lit rock of Acro Corinth
flash of white wing on the black window,
figures waiting by the door to the world.

Surrounded by the sweep of orange groves
painted booths line the sacred way,
women on their knees whispering Aphrodite
stirring a dark perfume in the deep green leaves.

From Hotel Shadow on the edge of spring
the utilitarian stables of Euro business
fall away to the gulf of crowded boats,
transporting televisions, cars and kitchens.

The lower world cracks apart on successive days
and we open casks, cups and pots in turn,
I think this is before the church, for Dionysus—yes yes,
Dionysus in flight from winter making us mad.

\*

The earth cracks in season
and memory set aside rises
by generation, vivid, unchanged.

I think he died in great pain,
drinking aftershave—old spice
and boot polish—on parade.

Are such themes found in folk song?
I don't know. Who is singing?
It's just the nature of the alcoholic.

But I am fifty now and still
I can barely tell you,
here's the last line, I made it.

\*

February is the month of the dead
the month of purification

the wine god in his garlands
flirts and slips and stumbles

the earth parting for the eager dead
they come from another country to have their fill

we are not who we seem
we don't sing what you think

\*

They lived in a village in another country
my mother would pick out its tunes,
hymns by ear, forgive our foolish ways
—well someone should, and laugh like a girl.

Lead kindly light between the wars,
her father built a business, fruit and veg to market,
all gone in the fatal crash on early morning ice
and the children taken in by relatives.

And before him the journeyman tailor,
a tall, dark man from Slad the narrow valley
and tight mouth, his wife from Bisley,
an even meaner place if possible.

I know them only by her stories
and she's been dead more than twenty years,
they set out across Hardy's fields,
their rough old songs beating in the heart.

*

And dancing uncle is pregnant with a balloon,
he leads his son the satyr with lopsided breasts,
and his daughter, Happiness, skips in circles laughing;
tomorrow is Clean Monday for vegetables and fish.

No—your feet like this, two two, one one, you lead
for Anthesteria, the days of risen ghosts about the city,
let me daub the doors with pitch and chew the buckthorn clean.
Souls—you've had your dish of grain and seeds—now go, now go.

Plastic trumpets and party poppers announce
you can beat Mr Death with a squeaky hammer,
hit him hard and run around the busy tables;
uncle gives birth to a goat, here's the skin to wrap you up in.

# News of Aristomenes

'...and the gods would be kinder to them because they were defending their
own and not committing a first injustice.'

—Yanni, what do you know about Aristomenes?
—Hmm, not too much... we could Google it.


1

I am Aristomenes of Andania and I will tell you everything,
what I did and did not do, how I invented the moment of decisive action,
the birth of fear which clears a field of men, Messenia of Laconians
—that was the history of the second rebellion.

What in the world would make me leave my village?
The buzz of bees, my olives fattening like black jewels,
the wagtail patrolling my patch in familiar light,
though the wind plays naughty in the Stenyklaros Valley.

It's true I refused the title of king, I accepted Captain,
I keep close to the men and their leaders, keep them even closer to me;
I can spot the traitors and be magnanimous, for others to deal with
and roll them in a ditch for pigs to snout out and feast on.

It's also true I ran once, from those bastard godly twins,
that doubling of them, against one mortality, defeats me;
I ran, I lost my shield, they may have been in a tree, or hovering
in my mind all along, in an empty sky, dread undid me.

They hail me three times Hekatomphonia—well, so it is then,
I am spattered in their red words up to my elbows;
a fox at the chickens makes feathers fly, and a little blood travels far
—of course a fox can slink out of the mouth of hell and look smart.

It's true I stole into their capital and laid tribute to Athena,
I danced into their heart, the brazen chamber, how flashy, how dazzling;

I laced their gruel with panic that morning, the streets trembled:
war's in the mind, I invaded theirs, my mouth's a weapon.

The stories of my charmed escape from capture are all true,
the stories of my escape from death are all from my mouth.
Think, no man returns from below ground. Have you talked to him?
Shared a drink? Held his hand and felt its warmth? No, I think not.

Yes I did consult the oracles, sources of power I plugged into;
the making of a secondary meaning has a single edge: action.
The dark contract, unseen, unspoken, of the earth, I know what I want,
you know the names of my victories and they will not be forgotten.

As for the mysteries, like a snake even nonsense bites, mock as you might;
the matter of my birth is secret, what I buried on Mount Ithome is not,
who knows what happens if you sleep in the narcotic shade of the fig?
the old goddess may rise a girl, trees thicken, the stream run fresh.

From the beginning there have always been stories about me,
I uphold the oracles of Lykos and I will recover Messenia;
my watchers are out on the hills and I'm ready,
I am Aristomenes of Andania and I will tell you everything.

2

In the bar opposite the Blue Café
from the heart of mechanical song
why not why not why not take time out,
this is what comes of beating pretty on a log.

There's a kiosk and a prize grab cabinet,
you can win a pink dolphin, a bear, a gold watch,
you can see the sea through a glass cube, the sea dancing,
where we parade sunlit after the earthquake.

Off Navarinou the Ottoman fleet goes down,
Gregory Peck steps up—don't argue with fire power,
in town three pyramidal wedding dresses in a row
prepare to go ballistic, lick of smoke whispers 3 2 1.

Finally on Shoe Street, the oral tradition is fixed,
SOUTH EMPIRE rises a line of fortified cities,
a realignment of the world, we have photographic proof,
ends in a fault running down Aristomenes.

*

According to Herodotus Aristagoras said to the Spartans—the Messenians have no gold or silver, or anything worth fighting for. So why should you bother fighting them? Go get the Persians. The Spartans did not listen and Aristomenes stepped forward.

*

We stayed two nights in the Hakos Hotel, Kalamata. It's on the seafront, scene of the allied rout in World War 2. As the Nazis bombed and strafed the crowded beaches the sea ran red with the blood of British and Commonwealth troops. They headed down into the Mani for evacuation to Crete. In the small harbours the dilapidated ships were bombed repeatedly and, although not hit, collapsed from the vibrations in the water.

We watched a film in the Hakos Hotel. Bruce Willis set out to rescue some good Africans from some bad Africans. There was talk of mineral rivalry. In fact Bruce's mission was to helicopter out a white doctor, she was French but with American citizenship. Bloodied Bruce, heroic maverick, went against orders; he wasn't meant to save non-Americans at all. The advert break on Greek TV is long and I was able to go down five floors, buy beer at the kiosk and return before Bruce resumed bleeding and rescuing liberally.

*

To test the endurance of the oral tradition and the life of myth I was thinking what to ask in Andania, where Aristomenes may have been born perhaps 2,600 years ago. 'Messene: A Dream Come True' by Eva Maria Leng and Waltraud Sperlich speaks of the Messenians as a people seeking and dreaming a homeland, drawing parallels to migrant workers in contemporary Europe. It espouses romance, destiny and ecology with the unsuppressed mood music of the great homecoming. I think it must be written for idiots, tipped that way. The 3D postcard of Delphi is more useful. The picture has a fine corrugated surface, like a mechanical sea in regulated waves. Tilt it one way the ruin of the site is seen, then at another angle the theatre is restored and time dismissed; an illusion printed in ridges. Remember Pausanias—'These are the stories; believe one or another according to which side you want to be on.'

*

In Messene the stone base for a bronze statue was discovered built into the wall of the apse of the basilica. The inscription is ΑΡΙΣΤΟΜΕΝΗΣ. By the 4th century A.D. the city was abandoned, ruined by the collapse of Rome, earthquakes and barbarian raids.

*

And then a morning so fresh
like a massive wet diamond
suspended above the white sea

with the tatty mimosa blowing and
the container ships stuck on the water
we went off around Taygetos
tottering and twisting in the air.

*

Mount Ithome folds itself around Messene,
layered blue hills, undulant olive trees white and green
roll out beyond sight to the plain and Spartan wall;
the city a natural amphitheatre, Hippodamian and mighty.

In founding Messene, above all they sought Aristomenes,
invoked and asked to return and dwell with them;
hillside rubble and scrub, bare earthworks, postholes,
roots turned over, the light invades every mote.

All the birds of Mavrommati sing and gentle rain rains down,
music falling in a green chamber for the river god of Pamisos;
from good red soil, over buried pillars, anenomies, hyacinths, daisies,
Oh Artemis on a bed of vetch most purple.

Later Melanie said—that flower we saw everywhere
that was mallow, sort of mauve, just everywhere;
and above all, at this point in the poem, I wanted to tell you
exactly what was there, unintoxicated, in April, recovering.

3

The best of it was our night raiding with the Fox,
blood released runs like black soup in that pitch;
with his rage on him he was a sight to behold
but once you looked there was no unseeing then.

It was a sort of sacrifice gone wrong, like butchery
the soft plopping of purple organs, knotty innards
by way of knife and spike onto our innocent soil,
eviscerate steam rising like a shitty ghost.

Hekatomphonia means we always counted the dead,
if you don't count the dead the dead don't count,
like in the kingdom of the two rivers, remote slaughter
remains on the eye and a terrible blindness is born.

We would slip out of Ithome into the arms of darkness
and everything smelt good, the fields in perfumed waves;
we were like kids rolling around a herb garden,
rags wrapped around our blades for silence ungleaming.

They would stand in dumb rows at a stockade—ripe for slitting,
or we'd catch a troop in a narrow pass and open the last gate for them.

*

He certainly did steal into Sparta one night, disguised,
right into the temple of Athena, bronze chamber, keeper of the city,
and laid his shield in tribute, as if from another world;
as intended, terror fell on the Laconians, like a knife to the bone.

He came trotting back after the mischief that morning and told us;
he had a charming tongue and could undo ropes and women with it,
you might ask Archidameia about this, devotee of Demeter etc,
she released him, covered her tracks and off he went like a boy in Spring.

You could also ask that farmer's daughter, she dreamt of him
and he turns up captive to a gang of Cretan archers, and again
the woman sets him free, and off he went driving out Laconians;
we wrecked their markets and made riot, whole areas abandoned.

He was chief kidnapper, cattle raider, three times hekatomphonia,
we sang that streets would be named after him, in Pherae say;
he knew the meaning of action like a distinct language,
he was the tin-sheet Andanian mystery boy and, as it goes, our saviour.

When it was all up he did the right thing by us, our captain;
we went into dread exile, some place—Zancle, Sicily—to the west.

\*

They would have us kill for words but you can take the story
as you see fit; whether the fool floated down borne by an eagle
or his shield let him bounce like a little lamb is unimportant;
the point is he returned and killed lots of Laconians.

They say there was something strange about him from birth,
he was favoured, his mother slept with a god in the likeness of a snake;
well that's pretty special—no wonder there were stories about him,
they talk and talk and he did all those things.

If he walked into town everyone downed tools, ribbons and flowers
    would fly,
the women would start singing impromptu, raising the dust and the rest;
he fought at all those places, Boar's Grave, Great Trench and led us out
    of siege,
we weren't serfs then, backs bent in the fields for another's tragedy.

That winter snow sat on the mountains all around us, a white bowl;
the river beds flooded and froze and old ones died by thin fires,
shadows of clouds like bunched black fists fell on the hills again and again;
he led us out of siege, in a spear shaped column we tore through
    Laconians.

I know another thing too—at the end of defeat he went to Rhodes;
he was old, he thought of Sardis, of Ekbatana, and died.

4

Aristomenes hunted Laconians on the plain and high mountain
Aristomenes went into Sparta at night, left Spartan spoil in Sparta's heart
Aristomenes laid his shield in the bronze house temple for Athena
Aristomenes went into Argos and Arcadia, allies and exiles returned
Aristomenes charmed Demeter's priestesses and escaped to Ithome
Aristomenes believed in the execution of memorable action and terrorising
    Laconians
Aristomenes fought at the Boar's Grave at the Great Trench and escaped
Aristomenes and his 300 stole corn, cattle and wine and drove the
    enemy out

\*

When the Spartans came over the mountain
and made us their slaves,
self appointed lords of the way it is
with their global credit, pipelines
and smart weapons in phalanx,
our irrelevance came to an end.

The hills at a certain hour turned mauve
and these men emerged in our fields
as if out of nowhere, clouds around their thighs,
their mouths barking—Helot—Barbarian—Outdweller;
they made Leuctra into an arms dump
and the crypteia proved themselves at night.

We had invented six languages in the dust,
mastered the olive, grape and grain
and tied the knots in an epic poetry;
on discs of light dropped by the gods
we walked the broken path of the sea
and still knew the songs the birds sang.

Your picture of the world can be undone,
stations off the air, iron ore shipped out;
the sky as blue, the terraces of the sea rise and fall
enough to break your heart each morning;
we no longer walked the ground,
the earth a shadow for another's empire.

*

Aristomenes has been thrown into deep Keadas and left for dead
Aristomenes has floated to the floor of the chasm on an eagle's spread
       wings
Aristomenes glides in the bronze light of the eagle on his shield
Aristomenes has drawn his cloak over his head and is waiting to die
Aristomenes has woken up to see a vixen nosing at corpses
Aristomenes has followed the vixen out of the shadows step by step
Aristomenes has been dragged by the clever one to the light and to Eira
Aristomenes went down into death and came back after three days to Eira

5

Aristomenes buried [the thing?] on Mount Ithome
[    ] what   [  it . . . .] was        [was]

Andanian        [                                    ]
[unknown] tin sheet – mystery     stamp[ed]

brazen chamber, bronze jar and [inside]
beaten to fineness [there was] a scroll

rescue  [                   ] old woman, you see
inscribed    goddess              the Great [one]

from her [hands]              instructions
[after death]   how           [to live]

            *


(To do the right thing even in defeat
Aristomenes buried the thing on Mount Ithome,
defeat as inevitable as the wild fig
bending to the stream or an oracular pun.)

            *


Cities buried, walls gone under meadows
olive groves over sanctuaries

they talk and talk
and the mountain grows

Meligala—on the upper or northern Messenian plain
—honeymilk

In Pig Valley, thick with trees, dark all day
—a sanctuary of Artemis

the names: marrow in the white bones.

*

Aristomenes buried the thing on Mount Ithome
Epaminondas dug it up after centuries
drew a circle on the ground, drew in streets and walls

*

Messenians absent for 300 years

did not change their customs
nor lose their Dorian dialect

rain-broken, thunder-broken
the white bones

*

And they went to Zancle, Sicily
the west darkening, the record dim

>	short is the way
>	and our Lady golden
>	long is the way
>	and our Lady golden

the Greeks there sing songs of the xenitia
of living away, to the north, to the factories

from 800 BC in Salento, Calabria and Sicily
Doric still spoken from a 6,000 word lexicon

Doric spoken valley to valley
villagers untouched by writing

    Oh my beautiful Morea
    I will not see you again
    I have my father my mother my brother
    all buried in the earth here
    I will not see you again

old woman climbing steps
       the Great One        a girl
from her hands   the song
       our Lady golden

*

In Andania the tattered banners proclaim
the perpetual season teased by the wind, a dog,
it could be new year—may you have many years.

The dog tears another strip and it could be
Easter for the god risen indeed
or No Day for victorious defeat.

Time sits by the road smoking
 the bus is late and there's no post,
Aristomenes sits by the road breaking empires.

## 6

I sit in the shade of this fig-tree
and wait and watch in the still air

washed from the backward turning sea
blue mountains fade in the haze

moment by moment the many words for light
rise, enough to hide a whole country

she laid the path over rock over water
everything I did she held in her hands

they will return from there
eyes gone dark with seeing

nearby a woodpigeon calls and
small birds sing in a chamber of sound

chirrup nations of chaos chirrup
a message draining the secret meadows

but slowly through the afternoon
the bronze bowl of silence fills

over there they are building
after fire and earthquake and war

tap tapping away for hope
shaping stone time will pock

                      \*

The fact white hot and near silent
in the squares and streets of Eira,
burning like a chamber of fire or forge
for making swords, proving men.

At the heart of it Sparta,
can only make itself in other lands
can only enslave, stamping Sparta
on strangers' faces in rows.

At the heart of it system collapse,
weapons technique, hidden deals,
the abduction of women and
cattle raiding dreamed night-long.

Fire makes a mirage of walls and towers
the sea sounding in a tunnel of
turning air, those voices high in Taygetos
fall upon us to map the risen world.

*

With morning coming over the roof
shadow falls on shadow to disappear,
something has driven the world into this
dark pilot of the course taken.

Self-appointed arbiters squeak by rote
—if it is fragmented, inchoate, so it must be written:
baleful Anacreon, get out of it,
go learn the song again.

Light steps over the roof, shadow on shadow,
war reports shake the air, wave after wave
piling up women and children in mounds;
this is what we do, only the names change.

We didn't stop from raising Messenia
lest Spartans took exception;
we hit hard, employed art, watched the hills
waited their approach—and for what?

The tangle of branches on the wall
a language, trace its slow progress;
the cicadas dry music its signature,
day advances, all meaning's changed.

   *

What I do is sit under the fig-tree and wait
at the point of death everything comes to life,
time stops and then whips, on the crumbling edge
of Keadas, birds wheeling below.

It might be a gentle wind lifts your sleeve
fresh as my love's breath, the light shows through
each fibrous thread, like wings extended
and their hands on your shoulders push.

The unimaginable darkness breaks out then,
in the pine trees bending and scattered rocks
whiteness pushing up through scrub,
rats, jackals, birds and frogs swoon to earth in a rush.

As in battle, it breaks out, blood leaking
from a young face, close up, the black hair soaked,
it all snaps shut, silence, and then the roar exalting,
a town goes up in smoke, a gleaming pile of spoil.

I sit, I wait, they keep the noise down around me,
dust falls in dark rooms, the sea nearby translates time;
smiling physicians appear through the curtains,
I expect a song and dance routine of sorts.

   *

She sings in the morning in and out of the kitchen
as birds sing because the sun rises
saying I was awake late last night,
her mouth opening and closing in yellow light.

I've returned several times from where there is no singing,
from Keadas, from Trophonius and at Leuctra, to Spartan frenzy;
they will call me exegete of the katabasis, or some such,
and each time there was never a girl singing like this one.

You have to go there and strike a dark bargain,
lie down, hold barley cakes mixed with honey,
go feet first into a mouth in the earth and shoot away
as if caught in a river, a river of blackness covers your head.

The return is difficult and never the same route as the descent,
I scratched a few words in seeds and blood on the passing rock;
she laces the air with her singing, there's a lucky boy in the village
and bees drift through clouds of flour as she claps and claps.


*Coda*

Even before Lycurgus launched Year Zero
and exported familial sadism as empire
everything unfolds in the high meadows
of the Hellenic subduction zone, its music
travelling westward at 3.5 mm per year.

Leonidas' palace is a casino of vanilla and gold,
the taxis of Sparta are red with white roofs
and snow shines its April message from Taygetos,
against the wall of that wall the sea a bloody memory
of Aristomenes sword dancing on the other side.

The language of action has dropped us here,
the forces of Anatolia, Africa and Eurasia
converge, grind and slide under our feet,
if the roaring speaks another poetry
a head lifts up pouring roots and red soil.

# On the Xenophone Label

# Propositions 1

On the Xenophone label
crackling late at night
from the outpost  barbarians in the hills
at the beginning as one

*

That these fossils prove
the earth was once sea
my eye on the substance
the whole world one god

*

What men think they know
is no more than the impulse
of frogs gathered around a puddle
singing late into the Spring night

*

From Syracuse Dear Parmenides
the sun is new every day
the sea has covered the land bridge
and the clouds ignite by motion

*

The limits of human knowledge
do not excuse inquiry
you are not off the hook
the rim of the world burning

*

The roots of the earth
and the unharvested sea
are above Tartarus the fool knows
set forth from Colophon unmapped

*

Religion makes men hungry
they sing pray parade up and down
then crowd the taverna their shiny faces
take eat take eat the whole world

*

In this airy space unconfined
I was not Homer's boy
I was not a mouth for hire
amber set fast about my buzzing words

*

In the chapters of sweetness
yellow honey gods made figs
made all things clear
iambic frogs meteors first principles

*

Empirical root holds true
thus I in rhapsody
at the edge of the dark sea
saw the town of men wake to light

*

Not plague nor Harpagus
but mumbo jumbo mytho Pytho
brings down the city
bang bang you thought wrong

        \*

And with my own eyes
silver jackal black snake
green lizard spring I saw
all things with my own eyes

        \*

At first I heard the name
Xenophanes of Colophon
middle up middle down
the music of reason Xenophanes

# A Biography of Xenophanes

Son of Dexus or Dexinos or Orthomenes
against Homer
against Hesiod
against Pythagoras
outlived his sons
defender of the city

Gadfly of Ionia, Sicily, Italy
gadfly against false wisdom
inquired into meteors, eclipses
fishes whirlwinds religion
the shape and location of the Earth
the substance of all existing things

inquirer into moderation of conduct

# Greetings 1

Parmenides my friend when
did we last speak how
are you and the horses and
your straight purpose I
am variously employed
in the many Greek lands
to make a living away
from home observed fact
came to call this morning
a warm wind of ignition
stirred the endless sea was
once land and my mind turned
to you in the market place
fresh melons that day off
the boat their liquid knock
as they collide caused an
argument atoms at war the
language of thirst exploded
one combatant quoted your
sharp mind like a knife
melons rolling everywhere
thuk thuk percussion subtle
as honey in sunlight a riot
you recall that day when
unmediated Harpagus
drove us westward the tide
the counter tide turns how
long do you think what is it
in such abandonment my
whole life strung out on wires
rigged the journeys made
lucid sea lanes of the
objective case a marvel
of song imagine song spun

around the earth even as
this letter beats its path
to you there's lightning
out on the waves revelation
along a long tunnel of
sound flooded the harbour
physis a chamber of noise
to knock me down the world
abides no less I saw one
moment the burning map
fire walking on water
they say that once sap
from pine bacchants of
pine in the air around the
house the voice and clatter
of gods they say
a voice in the resinous
body of night of earth
articulated a thesis
rising in a sort of song.

# Biography 2

Only poetry can do this
from an island invaded
by the world   only poetry
to the west Greek earthed

Xenophanes came here
his eyes open he walked
through the valley of temples
followed by twenty dogs

Thought sharp at first light
reverence   scepticism
opened his eyes on an island
of white marble Aegean

The cypress the mimosa
the fluted columns rose
from the same impulse
Xenophanes first saw this.

## Propositions 2

Number magic is as useful as
a dog barking in the early hours
there's nothing to steal here
only sanctimonious cant

*

Men's heads     melons
inside secret wet flesh
thinking: thuk thuk?
judged by action—who can say?

*

Let's talk of the old days in
Colophon when the hexameters
ignited first thoughts and we stood
together in the innocent air

*

Saw a kingfisher flash
green fire low on the water
in the still air of the harbour
nothing of earth about it

*

Black is their new purple
they crowd the market conjure
an empire of denial  magazine hair
oh but I am not interested in this passing world etc etc

*

The usefulness of fruit
as analogous to men
may be limited however
melons are less dense

          \*

The old women sit out
in the slow evening talk
eat they might sing float
away over the dark mountains

          \*

Up in the western market early for
weapons systems a new dawn
effaces an ethical consideration
holy script written in blood—yours

          \*

The sea beaten out silver
surrounds the children's dark heads
bobbing in family groups
their likeness—another message

          \*

Whispered in schools sung from towers
at dawn by rote in the blood
repeated in the houses of power
dog barking sanctimonious cant

          \*

To think with darkness abroad
the whole world but one constant
oh my drowned friends all
lost in the bloody roots of reason

*

The local bees here are black
heavy hanging in the yasmina
even the little white stars come
spinning down to earth from the earth

*

post-Eleatic clean out of memory
1 earth  2 water  3 sun  4 return
= the moist ground of we who come into being
Gaia 1  2  3  4 ends up Gaia

# Biography 3

The idea shone like static in his mind
as bright as 92 summers in the Greek lands
as morning rolled out to claim its origin
and the seas and rivers exhaled the balmy night.

Watching the shadows run to ground
he thought of the visible, the uncontained,
reason fighting upstream on an ordinary day
as a boy where he stood in the land first lost.

Orchards of cherry trees, silver traced in white rock,
there is one source—constant and the same—
the conflict of interest is real enough,
their mouths big and slack with wealth.

What age were you when the Mede came,
when the sea invaded the land and left its mark?
Image of seaweed, a fish in the quarries at Syracuse,
a bay-leaf print deep in Parian marble.

# Greetings 2

Parmenides the Eleatic sun
has hammered my brain shut
beaten flat the mountains and sea
to an oily picture of nothing
in a white hot squint I saw
the village idiot bring the news
he held up a letter and showed
all of us pointing at the black
headlines given the way it goes
he's the best messenger we have
look it says cynical butchers
revenge comes to roost blah the
blah bosses emblazon power on
shiny coins like miniature shields
hoarded in darkness their
commerce but war by another
name the world will end because
of a, b or c or any combination
of private armies skulk in the hills
eyeing up the port for a, b or c
the night barely dissolved at dawn
the tradesman arrive singing
the dogs barking loop the loop
dive under the donkeys kick up
biting the tassels choral yelps
you want these onions this pot
you sure want this cure make her
love you all night everything moving
against everything and the children
chase the dogs the mothers scream
from the yards the men shout
what is going on how can I
pray for a rent cut with all this
fucking noise it is a perfect model

of the One morning stark
the idiot can explain the lot
my brain as I've said is shut
the work comes and goes
the Big Idea holds true
I tote it about the dusty circuit
slip and slide drink the lord's wine
eat at his fat-faced table you want
this thought this lesson on human
understanding everything knocks
against everything the mighty hymn
of substance thuk thuk you know
the verb in Homer designates
the reaching of the water up to
Tantalus' chin and the action
of the waves warding off snowflakes
we're up against it   the world
of land and sea that lies all
about us   there   that's it   picture
me   mouth open   just above
the rising tide of matter   talking

# Biography 4

After what should be talked about
had been talked about, the men were quiet,
at rest, fed and lounging.

The girl sang into the still night,
Xenophanes was not old then, the years fell away,
the experience complete in itself.

She stood amongst them in their woven garlands,
looking ahead, unabashed and beautiful
—there was no philosophy for it.

It would take 2000 years
for this moment to be understood,
no-one spoke, the distance held.

O mediatrix clemens, O Beatrice,
a girl floating to the shore
steps through the door into light.

# The End of It All

Plato's thought police and their like would not have it:
for espousing that the heavenly bodies are not gods
bent on doing only what is best Xenophanes would get
five years solitary and for its repetition—the chop.

How gentle is the exploration of the limits of human knowledge;
from inside such inquiry, a faint ghost in an empty land, we hear
a transparent whisper of almost nothing through another's history,
we're not even there and the imperial circus of claimants presses.

Exiled to the roadhouse circuit—stubborn, sceptical, unassigned,
Xenophanes saw one night the cold stars in a presentive sky,
heard the dogs barking tuneful nonsense village to village
and entered the network of the brimming world.

## Propositions 3

The invention of coinage
and Lydian luxury   retail
gone to hell in a handcart
prepared the ground for invasion

*

When I turned around
the garden's green shade
a thin green snake
whipped across my feet

*

At night two villages away
—who calculated the intervals?-
of perfect quarter tones  the east
calling home in the blood

*

The heat that summer
killed the cicadas stone dead
power trembling on the air
the mirage of harbour defences

*

My children in another land
my days are dust   stop
going around the Greek cities
to follow the money  stop

*

Anthropomorphic fallacy
eucalyptus bee dust sky
blue sky another house *agathon*
sing up little sparrow sing up

\*

The new wine of Elea is sharp
but softens the gathering night
as the memory of small fires
makes the sun rise every day

\*

The branches the limbs
of the celebrants surround my house
against divination fact finding
made me partisan of the One

\*

My hands deep in the logic
of our present language
a spring candid and common
others will come to unearth

\*

The honey-sweet wine
returns us to the earth
first light stumbling block
of the lower town in glory

\*

Champion of infinite logic
captain of the steady state
all things are one in Catana
running to the edge of knowing

*

During eruption and earthquake
they believe priests wrapped in smoke
take the clamorous crowd as teacher
lest the ground open and mean nothing

*

In the light of either 'into' or
'in' or 'to' earth (or the earth)
taken as head to foot
exact as human knowledge

# Notes

*FROM HERE ACCORDING TO JENKYNS*
Jenkyns is a translator of Sappho.

*EPICURUS IS MY NEIGHBOUR*
Anything remotely to do with Epicurus in this poem comes from Eugene O'Connor's translation *The Essential Epicurus: Letters, Principal Doctrines, Vatican Sayings, and Fragments.*

The epigraph 'Over the calm, clear shining water…' is an anonymous fragment in *Greek Lyric Poetry* by M.L. West. There are also versions of Alcman and Archilocus here. See also Pritchard, *The Ancient Near East*.

*THE ROADSIDE SHRINE*
The unattributed lines in part 3 are from Clement of Alexandria and P. Evdokimov in Timothy Ware *The Orthodox Church*, 1993.

*MY JOURNEY TO EURIPIDES*
Alexiares, the speaker, is my invention; the name means one who is opposed. See Pausanias, Thucydides, Euripides, Kerenyi on Dionysus and Jane Harrison on ritual. After defeat the Athenian soldiers were imprisoned on Sicily in the marble quarries. Reciting a few lines of poetry could win freedom.

*FROM ALEXIARES'S SEPARATE NOTEBOOKS*
For *kanun*, the law of blood feud, the canon of Lek, see Edith Durham's *High Albania*.

*ALEXIARES IN EXILE*
Martin Bernal is the author of *Black Athena: The Afroasiatic Roots of Classical Civilisation*, 1987. See Ovid's poems of exile. Nicos Xylouris was a Cretan singer. Songs by Theodorakis were banned during the Greek colonels' dictatorship.

*SEA TABLE*
See *Gemistos Plethon: The Last of the Hellenes*, C.M. Woodhouse, 1986.

*PYTHEAS*
See *The Extraordinary Voyage of Pytheas the Greek*, Barry Cunliffe, 2001.

Byron's Karagiozis
The idea that Byron was used as sexual bait for Ali Pasha, to win allegiance to the British cause in the conflict with Napoleon, can be found in Ian Gilmour's *The Making of the Poets: Byron and Shelley in Their Time*, 2002.

News of Aristomenes
The only sustained source for the figure of Aristomenes, scourge of the Spartans, is Pausanias. See also Daniel Ogden, *Aristomenes of Messene: Legends of Sparta's Nemesis*, 2004.

On the Xenophone Label
Sources include J. H. Lesher *Xenophanes of Colophon: Fragments: A Text and Translation with Commentary*, 1992; George Thompson *The First Philosophers: Studies in Ancient Greek Society*, 1955 and Sherod Santos *Greek Lyric Poetry*, 2005.

www.ingramcontent.com/pod-product-compliance
Lightning Source LLC
Chambersburg PA
CBHW031152160426
43193CB00008B/340